Hank's Pranks

By Cameron Macintosh

Hank loves to play pranks at home.

Hank, Fran and Glen have a snack.

Hank sticks a trick ant on Fran's snack.

Stan the dog looks on.

“Yuck, an ant!” said Fran.

“It is just a trick ant!” said Hank.

He cracks up.

Hank gets Stan's soft frog.

"Glen will get a shock
if he puts his hand
on this!" Hank tells Stan.

Yuck, it is Stan's soft frog!
We must stop Hank's pranks!

Glen puts a plump trick rat in Hank's cap.

Fran puts a trick black bug on Hank's lamp.

Hank comes in.

“You must put an end to your pranks!” said Fran.

“OK, I will stop!” said Hank.

“Thank you!” said Glen.

CHECKING FOR MEANING

1. Where did Hank put a fake ant? *(Literal)*
2. What did Glen put in Hank's cap? *(Literal)*
3. How did Fran and Glen feel about Hank's pranks? *(Inferential)*

EXTENDING VOCABULARY

pranks	Look at the word *pranks*. What are the sounds in this word? What other word in the story can mean the same as *prank*?
cracks up	What does Hank do when he cracks up? What is another way to say that?
plump	How many sounds are in the word *plump*? How many blends?

MOVING BEYOND THE TEXT

1. Why do people tell jokes and play pranks?
2. In the end, the kids agree to stop playing pranks on each other. Why is it important to be honest with your friends and family about what you like and don't like?
3. Have you heard the saying "laughter is the best medicine"? What does it mean? How do you feel when you laugh?
4. What makes you laugh? How can you make other people laugh?

SPEED SOUNDS

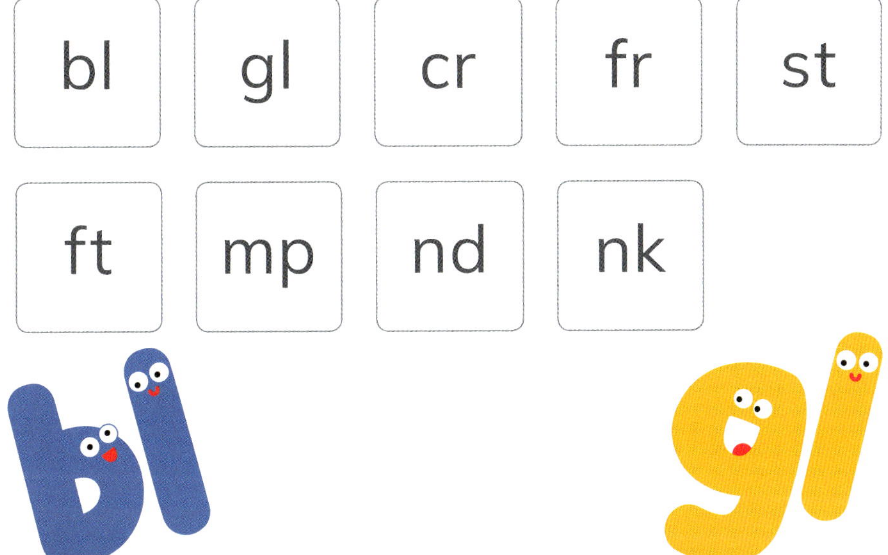

PRACTICE WORDS

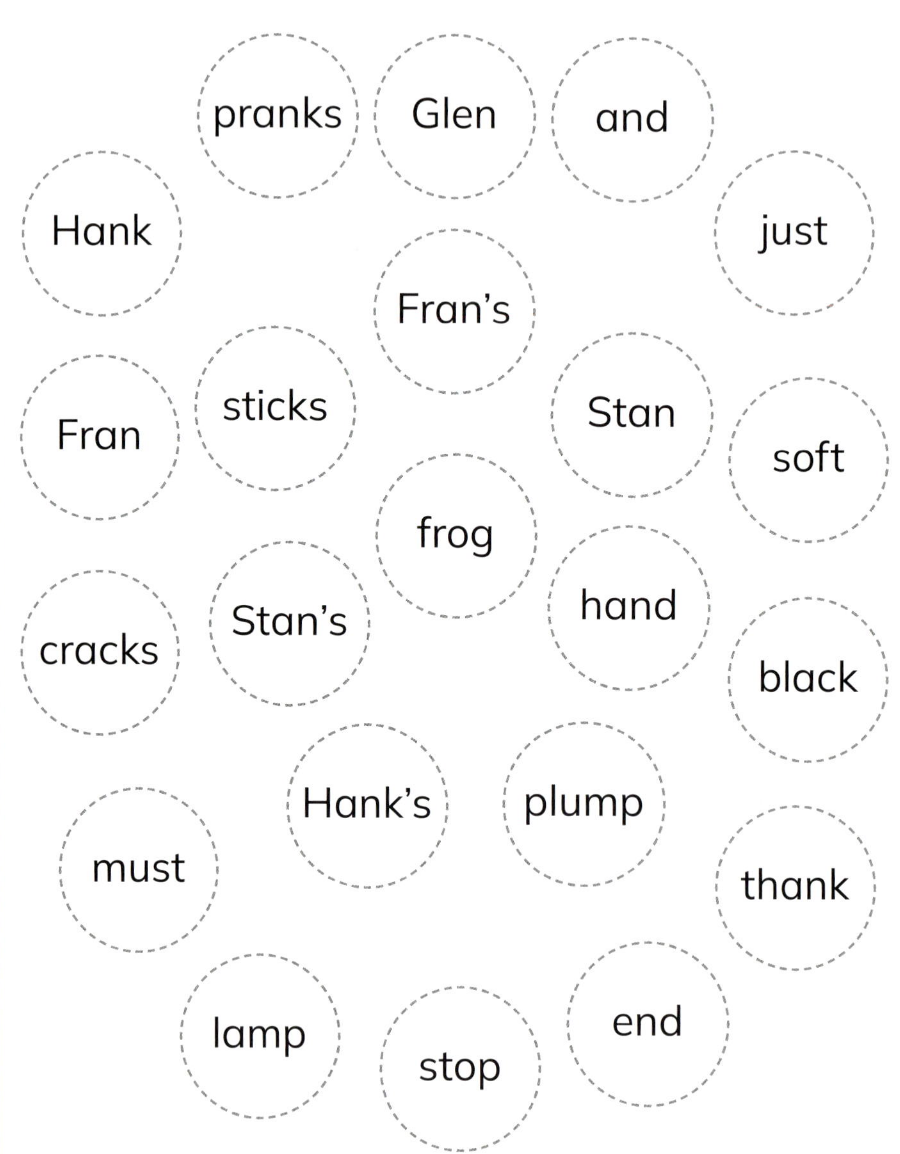